GW00836216

AOTEAROA

Aotearoa

A PHOTOGRAPHER'S JOURNEY AROUND NEW ZEALAND

Stuart Macdonald

Looking Toward Pirongia

Typical undulating farmland of the South Waikato as seen from the road to Kawhia on the west coast of the North Island.
The sun is coming through gaps in the clouds and lighting up parts of the scene. Mt Pirongia can be seen on the horizon at the far right.

Nikon D800E, 24–120mm at f8 and 1/140 sec. ISO 100.

CONTENTS

Old Pines in the Mist

A misty day on Mt Victoria, Wellington. It was near here that a number of *Lord of the Rings* scenes were shot. The mist swirls around the gnarly old pines and makes the place seem a bit eerie and other-worldly.

Nikon D800, 24–120mm at f11 and 1/30sec. ISO 400.

FOREWORD

A Photographic Journey

New Zealand is not just about beautiful landscapes, although there are plenty of those – it is also about the cities and towns and small localities that make up the country. Even though we are a relatively young nation there is a rich and friendly culture to be seen in the less usual places as you travel about. This book not only includes some of the traditional beauty of New Zealand but also attempts to convey to you, the reader, a wider range of images than you would usually see – images which draw out some of what is unique about New Zealand.

We are blessed within such a small country in having a wide range of landscapes and places all within an easy drive of each other. For instance one can enjoy the swamp forests of South Westland and then drive through the Haast Pass to the open semi-desert of Central Otago and the McKenzie Country. In the North Island one can explore the volcanic plateau and within a couple of hours be canoeing down the beautiful bush gorges of the Whanganui River.

We also have our 'quirky' New Zealand lifestyle, often easiest to see when driving through a small town. There may be a dairy open all hours, or the local pub, a community hall (or marae) or some old building converted to community use. Nowadays there will often also be a cafe for visitors – catching the tourist traffic that goes by. In the country side you may come across a 'weird' art piece at the farm gate or, in summer, a children's fruit stall. In a way these sorts of things are our true 'Kiwiana'.

As a 'young' country we do not have many truly old buildings – New Zealand was, after all, settled by Europeans only around 150 years ago, and by Maori some 700 years before that. There are a few old Government buildings to be seen as one travels around, but it is in the churches and original commercial buildings of both cities and towns that one can often see the old and the beautiful, or just how life was. Some of these old, unique or 'quirky' buildings are included here – to illustrate a New Zealand we often overlook.

New Zealanders love the open spaces, and have a strong history of exploring and enjoying our remote places. There are tramping tracks (although I am reluctant to call some of these proper tracks) and huts scattered all over our back country and national parks. New Zealanders also value their individuality, and you will see signs of this when you visit where they live – especially in small towns and localities slightly off the main road. They will have put their stamp on their piece of New Zealand.

The journey reflected in this book has taken place over several years. As I have travelled around New Zealand with my camera I have tried to capture these different elements of the country – from remote mountains and bush, to the beaches and lakes, to the places where people live. Although there are some shots of our traditionally beautiful landscape I have also wanted to show those less visited places – whether they be a beach on a stormy day, a remote place in the bush or high country, or an interesting old building somewhere – the 'ordinary' beauty of New Zealand. So in this book you will find a mixture of:

- beautiful traditional landscapes
- 'moody' or alternative landscapes
- 'quirky' small town New Zealand
- old or unusual buildings, or cityscapes.

Each of these images has a short 'story' telling the reader a little bit about the place (or how to find it) and maybe my reactions as a photographer being there – to help you also enjoy seeing what I and the camera saw.

About My Photography

Photography is a creative art that enables me to stop time – that is, to capture a moment or a place and preserve that for others to also experience. It is also about observation – about being connected and 'in the moment' of what you are doing, so that you 'see' at another level. For me 'observation' goes through several phases when I am taking a photograph – phase 1 is just finding the place or object and realising the possibilities; phase 2 is looking around to 'size up' the best angle or the light and phase 3 is 'composition' when I am refining how the image looks through the viewfinder.

At the start of each photograph (especially so with landscapes, or inside churches) I take the time to just absorb the place and the beauty that emerges. Often quite ordinary places can hide a unique beauty or image – such as the image of a local dairy or convenience store, or an old farm house. But one has to take the time to 'absorb' the place to see it.

Photography, particularly landscape photography, also involves patience – whether it is waiting for the light or coming back another time to get the right weather or sky. In this sense it is not unlike fishing, where a certain amount of luck helps and there might be days when you do not catch a fish at all.

The camera is an extension of my eye and my creative side. It not only captures the image but it also captures the essence of my thoughts and feelings as I took the shot. So for instance I would like to think the colours and shapes in a particular image convey for the person viewing it an emotional reaction to that place or object – just as when I was there taking the photograph.

For me the equipment (the camera) is only half of the photographic process. The other half is the person behind it. This means one has to be very familiar with the camera – to get the best out of it, especially in tricky lighting or weather – but equally one must practice 'seeing'. By this I mean stopping and being still. And just looking and imagining what images might be in front of you – observing and creating. So 'wandering around' whether in a town or in the countryside can open up possibilities, just like driving up a road to see what is at the end.

About the Future

It is part of our Kiwi nature to accept things at face value, to be reasonably direct, and to be open and friendly. For an overseas visitor it is often this friendliness, this simplicity, this slightly understated culture that makes their visit so rewarding. It is also part of our nature to respect the values and individuality of others, as long as they don't impact adversely on anyone else. However it is important to protect what we as a people value – to recognise what we have. There can be little doubt that some of our special places, and the localities close by, are under pressure. We need to do something about that.

I hope the collection of images in this book will help us to appreciate the beauty around us, and to value what we have.

Stuart Macdonald. 12 September 2019

Cape Reinga Lighthouse

Not quite the most northern part of New Zealand but close enough for photographic purposes. They say the confluence of ocean currents and winds around this northern tip of the country produces an interesting feeling to the place – and I think that is so. The wind rushes in, the sun shines fleetingly and the seas seem turbulent. It does feel different.

Nikon D750, 24–120mm at f16 and 1/45 sec. ISO 100.

Te Paki Sand Dunes

The huge sand dunes at Te Paki just south of Cape Reinga are really something quite different in terms of New Zealand landscapes. They are popular with people sand boarding, but there are whole parts of the dunes where few people go, and where you can experience the somewhat surreal exhilaration of walking these dunes. It is a fairly tough slog going up but once amongst the dunes you won't regret it. I wanted to capture the desolate immensity of the dunes, and I do think you get that feeling in this image. From the car park by the Te Paki stream just walk straight up and go from there.

Nikon D750, 24–120mm at f16 and 1/60 sec. ISO 100.

Ratana Church at Te Kao

Te Kao is in the 'far north' about 40 kms south of Cape Reinga. The church can be seen as you drive north on SH 1. In this image you can just see the five point stars and crescent moons atop each corner bell tower – Ratana symbols of light/enlightenment, and make out the words 'Arepa' and 'Omeka' which are Maori transliterations of the Greek words Alpha and Omega. The coloured star on the gate represents, among other things, the 'holy trinity' in Christian terms – Father, Son and Holy Spirit.

Nikon D750, 24–120mm at f16 and 1/90 sec. ISO 100.

Vote

This house is on one of the main streets as you enter Kaitaia. In a way it reflects the history of Maori grievance and activism that is part of New Zealand, and part of being in a functioning democracy where people can fight for justice and what they believe is right.

Nikon D750, 24–120mm at f11 and 1/250 sec. ISO 100.

Kaeo Cafe and Accommodation

Kaeo is a small rural town on the main road between Kerikeri and Kaitaia. This place has a 'quirky' style to it, and if you look closely you will see, amongst other things, the wooden eagle and rooster on the first floor balustrade. A good place to stop if you are travelling through.

Nikon D750, 24–120mm at f9.5 and 1/30 sec. ISO 100.

Mangroves Near Opua

There are many mangroves around the harbours and inlets of Northland. This image is an attempt to capture the 'mood' of the convoluted shapes as the mangroves stretch up out of the tidal waters.

Nikon D750, 24–120mm at f16 and 1/6 sec. ISO 800. Handheld. Shot taken at dusk to avoid harsh light and shadows.

In Waipoua Forest

The Waipoua Forest lies some 20 kms south of Hokianga Harbour and is home to some of the largest Kauri trees in New Zealand. But there are many beautiful parts to the forest and this image captures the luxuriant dense growth near one of its many streams. It has been raining and everything is wet – there is a slight 'shimmering' on all the leaves. In a place like this one has to be very watchful as there are steep drops into streams and gullies.

Nikon D750, 24–120mm at f13 and 1/8 sec. ISO 400. (Handheld – there is no easy placement of a tripod here.)

Kawakawa Toilets

The Kawakawa Hundertwasser toilets are famous, and very popular. In fact I had to wait patiently even though not a busy time of the day, in order to get this photograph. The idiosyncratic and colourful Hundertwasser style is really quite unique and Kawakawa has made a theme of this throughout the town.

Nikon D750, 24–120mm at f16 and 1/8 sec. ISO 400. Handheld.

On Kawakawa Main Street

Opposite the Kawakawa toilets is the Grass Hut shop, also in the Hundertwasser style, and beautifully done. In particular the mural on the side of the building is something to behold – above the first 'face' on the left end are the words 'Conservation is a State of Harmony between Men and Land'. Just to stand there and let your eyes wonder over the whole thing is a joy.

Nikon D750, 24–120mm at f11 and 1/180 sec. ISO 400.

NORTHLAND

Ocean Beach Near Whangarei

Whangarei is blessed with waterfalls, beautiful bush walks, a warm climate and so on. Also close by are bays and beaches that are typical of Northland – Ocean Beach is an example. Located down toward Bream Head and popular with surfers it does though feel isolated and remote (in fact it is a 5 minute walk from the small car park). This is the view if you climb up to the ridge at the south end of the beach. There is a smaller and even more private beach on the other side of the ridge.

Nikon D750, 24–120mm at f13 and 1/125 sec. ISO 100.

Smugglers Bay

Smugglers Bay is part of the Bream Head Scenic Reserve at the entrance to Whangarei Harbour. A short walk across local farmland takes you to the beach and, depending when you go, there may well be no-one else around. The much longer Ocean Beach is on the other side of the heads, and is not as sheltered and peaceful as here.

Nikon D750, 24–120mm at f16 and 1/125 sec. ISO 100.

Railway Bridge 178 Birds

Both side buttresses of the railway bridge have these lovely Kiwiana paintings on them – one of New Zealand's birds (this image) and one of New Zealand's flowers. Bridge 178 is just on the edge of the Whangarei CBD, and is easy to find. Each bird has a character as reflected in the Maori and English words you can see. For example the Kaha/Strength of the eagle.

Nikon D750, 24–120mm at f9.5 and 1/125 sec. ISO 100.

Pukenui Falls Whangarei

The A H Reed Memorial Park in Whangarei contains mature Kauri trees, including an elevated canopy type walk, but also the beautiful Pukenui falls (also known as the Paranui Falls). Getting to the base of the falls involves a bit of scrambling through the bush as the walking track takes you to the top of the falls and to the stream below only. But as you can see it is worth the struggle – the falls drop into a small secluded clearing surrounded by moss covered rocks. Even though only 15 minutes from the city CBD it feels like you are in the remote bush somewhere.

Nikon D750, 24–120mm at f11 and 1/8 sec. ISO 100. Handheld in order to get this angle.

Home Away from Home – Whangarei

When New Zealanders go on their summer holidays they often make their campsite quite unique – it is a time to relax and be yourself. Here is an example, admittedly at the more extreme end, but lovely just the same. One can enjoy, along with these caravan campers, some of their passion.

Nikon D750, 24–120mm at f13 and 1/30 sec. ISO 200.

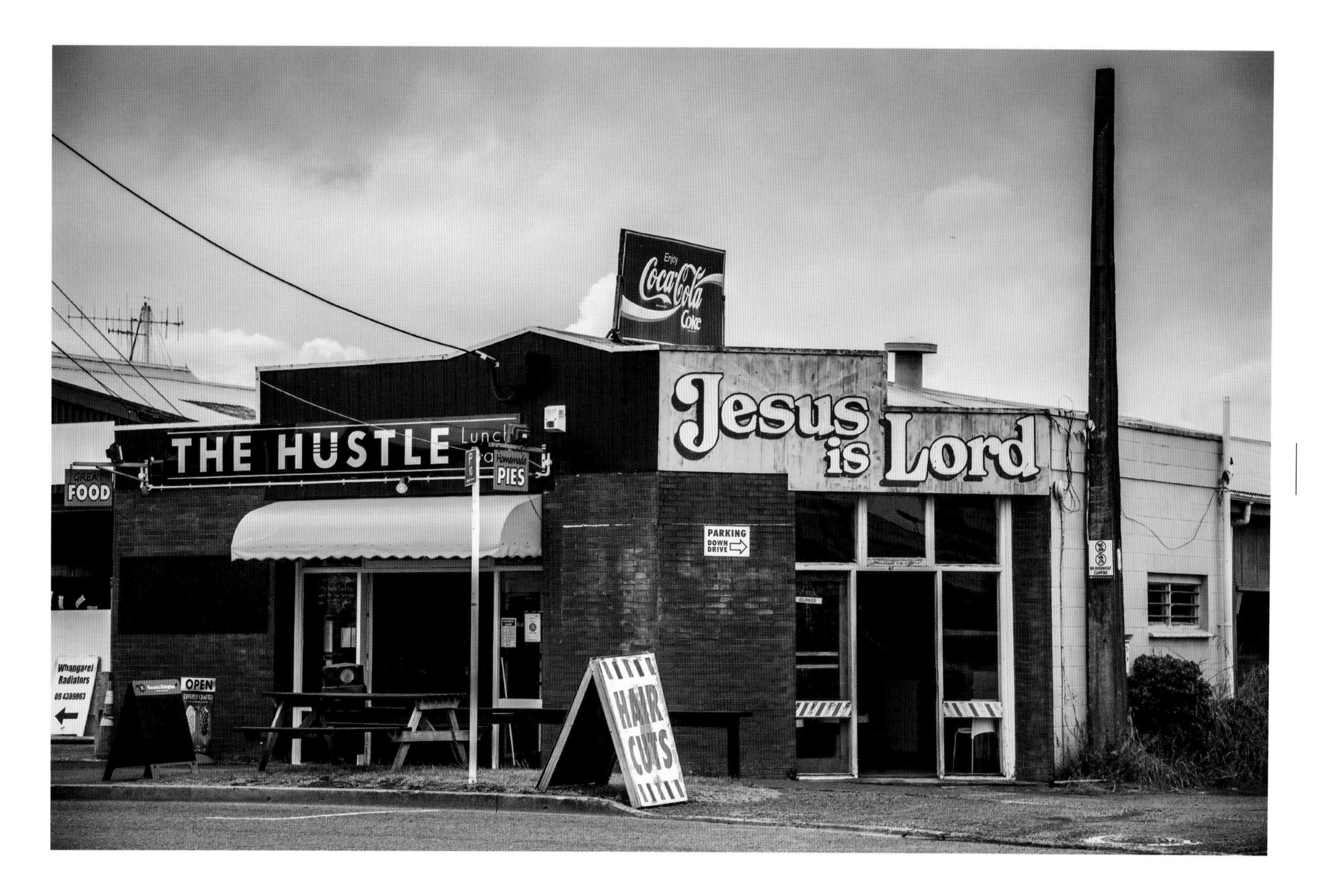

Mixed Messages

This is in the commercial area of Whangarei. The mixture of signs caught my eye as I drove past. On my count there are around 10 different signs, including 'Jesus is Lord'. I could not work out why that one was there, above the barber shop.

Nikon D750, 24–120mm at f8 and 1/125 sec. ISO 100.

Bubble Rocks at Sandspit

Sandspit is about one hour north of Auckland. It is one of those typical New Zealand summer holiday areas, and the camping ground has many quirky iconic baches, including some along the edge of the estuary. At low tide these rock formations can be seen just walking along the shoreline not far from the holiday park. The ferry to Kawau Island leaves from the Sandspit wharf nearby.

Nikon D750, 24–120mm at f16 and 1/60 sec. ISO 100.

Late Spring Day at Muriwai Beach

Muriwai Beach is a beautiful long 'black sand' beach on the Auckland west coast. Very popular with beach goers and fishermen. Here it is a late afternoon at the beach – in the distance you can see a boat being pulled out of the water and closer to the camera kids are sliding down the sand dune on the right, while others just soak up the last of the sun's rays. The rough Muriwai sea comes in against the rocks.

Nikon D750, 24–85mm at f16 and 1/8 sec. ISO 100.

Looking South from Flat Rock Muriwai

It is an invigorating feeling standing on Flat Rock, with the waves crashing about you – especially nearer high tide. Sadly fishers have been swept off the rocks and drowned so care is needed. Today it is not yet high tide and we can see the gannet colony off to the left of the image, and the cliffs to the south. Muriwai is one of those special New Zealand places, but take care around the rocks.

Nikon D750, 24–85mm at f16 and 1/180 sec. ISO 400.

Rangitoto on a Dark Day

Iconic Rangitoto can be seen from many vantage points and beaches around Auckland. In this image the dark clouds are reflecting on the slightly moving water so that one's focus is narrowed, and the clouds and water and Rangitoto seem to be all there is.

Nikon D750, 24–85mm at f16 and 1/125 sec. ISO 100.

Near Cheltenham Beach Devonport

There are some expensive houses around Devonport, and especially near Cheltenham Beach, but here is an unusual one – a small place with quirky garden ornaments. I, like many others I guess, especially like the attitude of the two dogs – and, of course, there is the giraffe in the background (you will almost see the gnome at its feet). Lovely.

Nikon D750, 24–85mm at f16 and 1/60 sec. ISO 100.

At Northcote shopping centre Auckand

New Zealand is an immigrant nation, firstly Maori, then European and now Asian. Auckland now has a high proportion of relatively recent immigrants, mainly from various Asian nations – Northcote shopping centre provides a colourful example.

Nikon D750, 24–85mm at f11 and 1/15 sec. ISO 400.

Harbour Bridge Light Show Auckland

These days the Auckland Harbour Bridge 'light show' comes on for special occasions. It really is worth catching if you can. A good spot, from where this image was taken, is at Northcote Point, just where the ferries leave for the city.

Nikon D750, 24–85mm at f8 and 10 seconds. ISO 100. On tripod with VR off.

Auckland Skyline at Dusk

In this time exposure the water has started to smooth out and the lights of the city are coming on. The ferries which run back and forth to the north shore suburbs have all docked for the moment. It is a beautiful (and changing) skyline.

Nikon D750, 24–85mm at f19 and 10 seconds. ISO 100. On tripod with VR off.

Britomart Station Auckland

The artistic potential of the new Britomart station captured me. Often much busier than this. The disks in the ceiling are shafts capturing the light from the street level above. The Auckland city rail system is continuing to be upgraded and there are signs of this construction in many places around the CBD area.

Nikon D750, 24–85mm at f8 and 1/10 sec. ISO 800. Handheld.

Abandoned House at Glen Afton

Around New Zealand many of the small mining towns have long since lost their mining families and now are home to people wanting a simple, lower cost life. There are often one or two abandoned houses left behind, and here is one. Glen Afton was once one of several thriving coal mining communities near Huntly in the North Island, but is now a quiet forgotten place.

Nikon D750, 24–85mm at f16 and 1/125 sec. ISO 100.

Otama Beach Coromandel

Otama Beach is north of Whitianga in the Coramandel.
It is one of those pristine white/golden beaches out of the picture books, with Pohutukawa trees dotted at points along the high tide mark.
It is a little bit off the beaten track and at this time of the year (not summer) is basically empty.

Nikon D800E, 24–120mm at f13 and 1/180 sec. ISO 100.

Cathedral Cove Coromandel

Cathedral Cove is idyllic, but very popular with visitors, especially in summer. If one is to avoid people on the beach or in the water then an early start or a sunny day in winter is the best solution.

Nikon D800E, 24–120mm at f9.5 and 1/500 sec. ISO 100.

Waikato River Hamilton

The Waikato River is the longest river in New Zealand, starting near Mt Ruapehu and flowing through Lake Taupo, and on through Hamilton (where this shot is taken) to the sea at Port Waikato. In Hamilton the river flows close to the CBD and there are many easy walks along its banks. Here the Claudelands Bridge can just be seen in the distance. It is hard to believe the city centre is only 2–3 minutes away.

Nikon D750, 24–120mm at f11 and 1/125 sec. ISO 100.

Indian Char Bagh Garden Hamilton

The Hamilton Gardens are rightly famous for their amazing themed gardens, much visited by locals and travellers. It is well worth the time to wander through (allow at least 2–3 hours if not more) to see immaculate representations of gardens from different times and cultures. At this time of the year the Indian garden is full of colourful flowers set into the ornate symmetry of the surroundings – it was a place of peaceful refuge for the rulers of the time, an escape from the somewhat frenetic and brutal life outside.

Nikon D750, 24–120mm at f16 and 1/125 sec. ISO 100.

Fantasy at Hamilton Gardens

A novel idea being developed at the Hamilton Gardens is the notion of a fantasy or surreal garden, and this shot of the 'Saucy Sue' is an example. The black and white treatment captures ones imagination more I think.

Nikon D750, 24–120mm at f11 and 1/30 sec. ISO 100.

Ohaupo Bowling Club

The bowling club has seen better days. The daisies and long grass cover the old bowling green.

Nikon D750, 24–120mm at f16 and 1/60 sec. ISO 100.

Water Tank

Somewhere in the Waikato on a cloudy, dismal day. In a way I think this captures rural New Zealand – well at least dairy country.

Nikon D750, 24–120mm at f11 and 1/250 sec. ISO 100.

Solitude

In this black and white image I wanted to capture a feeling – of aloneness, reflection and facing adversity.

Nikon D750, 24–120mm at f9.5 and 1/250 sec. ISO 100.

Kiwiana Otorohanga

Otorohanga is a country town on the border between the Waikato and the King Country.
It is a thriving, positive sort of place – as reflected in this wall mural.
I could not resist as this so captures Kiwi New Zealand culture.

Nikon D750, 24–85mm at f11 and 1/250 sec. ISO 100.

Fishing Spot Marakopa

An old fishing spot (or maybe whitebait?) near Marakopa on the wild west coast of the North Island. The Marakopa River is in the background and the beautiful Marakopa Falls are back down the road about 20 kms toward Waitomo.

Canon 600D, 18–55mm at f8 and 1/180 sec. ISO 100.

Phone Box Marakopa

An old phone box and satellite dish in remote Marakopa on the North Island's west coast.

Canon 600D, 18–55mm at f8 and 1/90 sec. ISO 100.

Abondoned Church – Whakatane

This old dilapidated church sits in a graveyard on the edge of Whakatane. It has not got long to go.

Nikon D7200, 18–105mm at f9.5 and 1/45 sec. ISO 100.

In the Redwood Forest 1

The Redwood Forest on the edge of Rotorua has many easy walks through the towering redwoods. I had been there several times hoping to catch a misty morning. Finally one arrived. It was completely still and quiet.

Nikon D7200, 18–105mm at f13 and 1/3rd sec. ISO 100. On tripod (VR off).

In the Redwood Forest 2

Here, in a small clearing, the Rotorua Redwoods are towering above you. The forest floor is bereft of any growth except, as in the case here, where a few hardy saplings begin to make their way upwards. There is something special about wandering around with these vertical trees soaring on all sides. It is a special place – just pick a time when not many people are around.

Nikon D7200, 18–105mm at f11 and 2 seconds. ISO 100. On Tripod (VR off).

Pulp and Paper Mill – Kawarau

The pulp and paper mill at Kawerau is a conglomeration of smoking chimney stacks, complicated looking towers, conveyers, curved piping and other structures. With the dark skies it all makes for a somewhat 'dystopian' feel to the place.

Nikon D7200, 18–102mm at f8 and 1/250 sec. ISO 100.

Otuwhare Marae Omaio East Cape

This beautifully looked after Marae is just south of Te Kaha on the East Cape road. If you look closely you will see the sun symbol over the entrance to the Marae – representing the birth and growth of mana (power) in the world. In Maori mythology it is said the world itself is created each morning with the rising of the sun.

Nikon D7200, 18–105mm at f8 and 1/500 sec. ISO 100.

Church at Waihau Bay

This is the historic Raukokore Anglican Church at Waihau Bay, East Cape. The church was built in 1894 and has survived the rigors of the sea and wind since then. If you look closely you can just see the support beams on the sides of the church. I wanted to capture both the church and the sea to convey a sense of strength and fortitude in standing against the elements.

Nikon D7200, 18–105mm at f5.6 and 1/500 sec. ISO 100.

Old Farmhouse Near Gisborne

There are still quite a few old abandoned farmhouses around New Zealand. Often they are used to store hay for winter – sometimes like this one, firewood on the front porch. This place is on the Whakatane to Gisborne Road about 30 kms out from Gisborne.

Nikon D7200, 28–105mm at f8 and 1/500 sec. ISO 100.

Hati Nati Cafe Ruatoria

If you travel around East Cape you are off the usual tourist path. Here in the small settlement of Ruatoria is the Hati Nati Cafe, but it was not open when we went past.

Nikon D7200, 18–105mm at f8 and 1/500 sec. ISO 100.

Tolaga Bay Wharf

A full exploration of New Zealand is not complete without a trip round East Cape. Here, off the usual tourist routes, is part of New Zealand that many don't see – rugged in places, and remote. The Tolaga Bay Wharf was, in earlier times, an essential part of economic survival for the area. Local initiatives have saved the wharf from deterioration, and it is possible to walk the 600 or so meters out to the end.

Nikon D7200, 18–105mm at f11 and 1/125 sec. ISO 100.

Muriwai Beach toward Young Nicks Head

This is the Muriwai Beach in the Poverty Bay, near Gisborne (there is more than one). I like the plain open lines of the image and the lighting on Young Nicks Head.

Nikon D7100, 18–105mm at f8.0 and 1/500 sec. ISO 100.

Aniwaniwa Falls

These beautiful falls are just a few kilometres on from Waikaremoana settlement. There are several waterfalls in the area, all easily accessible. This image was taken at the end of the day when the light was failing – a long shutter speed gives the water a milky look, and the green moss on the rocks is captured in the dimming light.

Canon 600D, 18–55mm at f16 and 3 seconds. ISO 100. On tripod.

Bush Toilet Ureweras

Bush toilets are found on many walking tracks in New Zealand, especially the more popular ones. Here is one in the Ureweras, on the Ruapani track.

Canon 600D, 15–55mm at f8 and 1/6 sec. ISO 800. Handheld.

Near Waitanguru King Country

On a back country road north from Piopio in the King Country one finds these rocky outcrops. Some *Lord of the Rings* scenes were shot nearby and there certainly is a slightly surreal feel to the rough rolling hills peppered with interesting shapes.

Nikon D800E, 24–85mm at f16 and 1/60 sec. ISO 100.

Ohura on a Sunny Day

Forgotten and peaceful – Ohura is 'off the beaten track' in the King Country about 30kms west of Taumaranui. Ohura was a thriving town of almost 700 people in the 1960s but once the coal mining ceased and the Prison closed its population dwindled – there are now around 100+ people living there.

Nikon D7200, 18–105mm at f9.5 and 1/250 sec. ISO 100.

In the King Country

The King Country is full of steep rolling hills, and when the sun starts getting lower in the sky the simple beauty of the hills becomes apparent to the eye. Here is a typical King Country scene near Taumaranui, taken in summer when there has not been any rain for a while – and the farmers are complaining about how dry it is.

Nikon D610, 24–85mm at f11 and 1/125 sec. ISO 100

Upper Whanganui River

Here is the Whanganui River as it wends its way through the King Country before entering the National Park further to the south. Many of the canoe trips down the river start from Taumaranui, near here.

Nikon D610, 24–85mm at f11 and 1/180 sec. ISO 100.

Lake Taupo at Dawn

Taken at the small settlement of Motuoapa just north of Turangi on the eastern shore of Lake Taupo, near the small marina and jetty. No-one is about – it is crisp and cold, frost is still on the ground.

Nikon D800, 24–120mm at f8 and 1/125 sec. ISO 100.

Emerald Lakes Tongariro National Park

The Tongariro Crossing takes you past the three Emerald lakes. Here, late in the day, most of the walkers have started their trek back down the mountain and you can enjoy the harsh beauty of the lakes more or less in solitude. The Oturere Valley is in the distance, lower down and to the right.

Nikon D800E, 24–120mm at f8 and 1/500 sec. ISO 100.

Oturere Valley

From the Tongariro Crossing track it is possible to walk down into the Oturere valley (part of the 'Round the Mountain' walk). Near Oturere hut there is a large 'moonscape' area of volcanic rocks of all sizes and shapes, in an arid, desolate landscape. In this shot we are looking toward the main craters of Mt Tongariro, with Mt Ngauruhoe out of view to the left.

Nikon D800E, 24–120mm at f11 and 1/30 sec. ISO 100.

Mt Ngauruhoe from Mangatepopo

It is still fairly early in the morning and has not warmed up enough to disperse the cloud and mist around the cone of Mt Ngauruhoe. From a small hollow off the walking track near Mangatepopo the imposing presence of the mountain is captured by the camera.

Nikon D800E, 24–120mm at f13 and 1/250 sec. ISO 100.

Summer Pool on Mt Ruapehu

Mountain lichens and mosses cling to the rocks and crevasses around a small pool of water high above the bush line on Mt Ruapehu.
In heavy rains or during the spring thaw water rushes down, polishing shapes into the rocks on the far side of the pool.
On a cloudy, misty day the subdued light makes for a quiet, desolate beauty.

Canon EOS M3, 11–22mm at f11 and 1/15 sec. ISO 100.

Pylons Near Desert Road

The sun shone for a moment on the harsh, windswept land off to the side of the Desert Road, and the pylons stood out like machines walking across the landscape. It was cold!

Nikon D800, 24–120mm at f13 and 1/90 sec. ISO 100.

Looking Toward Ruapehu and Ngauruhoe

If you travel up the Whanganui River Road through Pipiriki to Raetihi you will come across a view a bit like this about 12 km out from Raetihi.
Both Mt Ruapehu and Mt Ngauruhoe are crystal clear in the distance, under the cloud cover.
You will have to go up the side road and then walk into the hills a bit, but not too far, to get this view.

Canon 7D, 15–85mm at f8 and 1/500 sec. ISO 100.

Ratana Church at Raetihi

It has seen better days – but still captures the unique 'style' of Ratana churches. The crescent moon and five pointed star of Ratana can be seen – these symbolise enlightenment. Through its history Ratana has been both a church and a political movement.

Nikon D810, 24–120mm at f11 and 1/125 sec. ISO 64.

Whakaki Lagoon

This hidden place is off the Napier to Gisborne road just past Wairoa. After a scramble across the railway tracks (no longer used) and wandering around the edge of this huge lagoon one comes to this. The only noise is the birds.

Nikon D7100, 18–105mm at f9.5 and 1/180 sec. ISO 100.

Church at Omahu

As you come down off the Gentle Annie Road (Taihape to Napier) you strike the small community of Omahu – before deciding whether to go right to Hastings or left to Napier. This small church and the cemetery around it are right at the cross-roads. It is late in the day and the sky is especially blue.

Canon 7D, 15–85mm at f8 and 1/180 sec. ISO 100.

Letterboxes

Late in the day I stopped the motorcycle on the Weber to Dannevirke Road near Mangatoro. The low sun is shining on the letterboxes, lighting them up.

Canon 1000D, 18–55mm at f8 and 1/20 sec. ISO 100.

Te Mata Peak

The sun rises on Te Mata Peak near Havelock North in the Hawkes Bay. Like many landscapes this was dependent on the weather. There were several attempts to get the pattern of light on the slopes that you see here, but eventually it came together. Again, patience is rewarded.

Nikon D800, 24–120mm at f11 and 1/60 sec. ISO 100.

North from Te Mata Peak

The early morning sun is shining along the northern ridgeline of Te Mata Peak. In this view we are looking north out over Hawkes Bay with the Tukituki River to the right far below. Being early morning means that, apart from the odd mountain biker or walker, there is no-one else around and you can hear the faint noises of the world, as it starts its day, rising up from the distance.

Nikon D800, 24–120mm at f9.5 and 1/30 sec. ISO 100.

Old House Mono

North of Waipawa on the Wellington–Napier main road. There are still many old farmhouses scattered about the countryside – you just have to watch as you go by.

Nikon D800, 24–120mm at f9.5 and 1/125 sec. ISO 100.

Takapau Hotel

The country pub at Takapau in Southern Hawkes Bay.
It is like many country pubs with parking out the front and accomodation/rooms to let.
It is of course much busier on a Friday or Saturday night.

Canon 7D, 15–85mm at f8 and 1/90 sec. ISO 100.

Angel – Porangahau

While on a motorcycle trip around the Wairarapa and southern Hawkes Bay we stayed at the small coastal settlement of Porangahau. There are two cemeteries there – one Maori and one Pakeha/European. This lovely angel is in the Maori cemetery – she seems Polynesian to me.

Canon EOS–M, 18–55mm at f8.0 and 1/45 sec. ISO 100.

White Cliffs Revisited

On the Taranaki coast north of New Plymouth there is the White Cliffs walkway – but you don't want to do the walkway – rather, wait for low tide and walk along the narrow beach below the cliffs. You will be rewarded by spectacular cliffs and a feeling you are the only person on earth.

Nikon D810, 24-120mm at f16 and 1/45sec. ISO 64.

Tongaporutu

I had always thought that Tongaporutu on the North Taranaki coast would look darkly beautiful on a stormy, cloudy day. This proved to be so. At low tide the rocks and pillars are also surrounded by sea water pools, and all of this makes for an eerie melancholy beauty. This image shows the largest of the Sisters through an opening in the surrounding rocks. Access is by walking along the river to the beach at the river mouth, and turning left. This is an easy walk but can only be done at low tide.

Nikon D810, 24–120 at f13 and 1/30 sec. ISO 100.

Tongaporutu Three Sisters

This shot of the Three Sisters was taken at the same time as the one opposite. Here all three 'sisters' seem to loom over the scene, and the dark sky adds a sombre atmosphere. On a day like this no-one else is around. One can absorb the raw beauty of this place in a peaceful solitude.

Nikon D810, Samyang 14mm at f16 and 1/45 sec. ISO 64.

Road to Mt Taranaki

State Highway 45 takes you round Mt Taranaki via the coast – a trip that circles over half of this symmetrical volcanic mountain. Here I stopped the motorcycle near one of the many roads that lead across local farmland in a more or less straight line toward the base of mountain. I wanted to capture the feeling of the road receding into the distance – with a final destination as you can see.

Nikon D7200, 18–105mm at f9.5 and 1/250 sec. ISO 100.

Goblin Forest

The ethereal feel of the Goblin Forest only really emerges when the mist and drizzle swirl around the slopes of Mt Egmont/Mt Taranaki. This magical scene is on the Ngatoro Loop Track accessed via the North Egmont Visitor Centre.

Nikon D800, 24–120mm at f16 and 1 second. ISO 200. On tripod.

Clouds of War

Te Henui Cemetery, New Plymouth, has a large section devoted to remembering fallen New Zealanders who served their country in various wars. Like war graves everywhere there is row upon row of headstones marking the many who died.

Nikon D800E, 24–85mm at f13 and 1/180 sec. ISO 100.

Oanui Gas Rockets

The Oanui gas production plant is situated in the middle of Taranaki dairy country, near the coast and not far from Cape Egmont. It processes natural gas from the offshore Maui A platform. In the late afternoon sun the refining towers with their convoluted piping remind me of Flash Gordon and rocket motors and space ships.

Nikon D7200. 18–105mm at f8 and 1/500 sec. ISO 100.

Manaia Rotunda

Manaia is a small town west of Hawera in Taranaki. The rotunda is in the central square with the bread factory on one side and the pub on the other. The names of local servicemen who gave their lives are placed around the rotunda, and the cenotaph on the other side commemorates their sacrifice.

Canon 7D, 15–85mm at f8 and 1/90 sec. ISO 100.

Old Bones Patea

This shot captures the old derelict freezing works at Patea from across the river.
The combination of the driftwood and the abandoned works led to the title for this image.

Nikon D800, 24–120mm at f16 and 1/60 sec. ISO 100.

WHANGANUI

Whanganui River

The upper Whanganui River north of Pipiriki winds its way through bush covered gorges for some 40 km or so. It is a magnificent river with a glorious history – shaped by both Maori and Pakeha. This image captures the grandeur of the river, with its bush clad cliffs bathed in mist and the water moving quite slowly – an undisturbed serenity.

Nikon D810, 24–120mm at f6.7 and 1/30 sec. ISO 800.

Mangaio Gorge

On a grey misty day the steep bush covered gorges of the upper Whanganui River create a moody, soulful experience. The Mangaio Stream is one of many tributaries feeding in to the river and the entrance to Mangaio Gorge itself is only a few kilometres north of Pipiriki. It is really only accessible by jet boat or canoe – if you can keep the camera still enough you can capture an amazing image.

Nikon D810, 24–120mm at f9.5 and 1/15 sec. ISO 800. (A very steady hand and good Vibration Reduction lens are essential.)

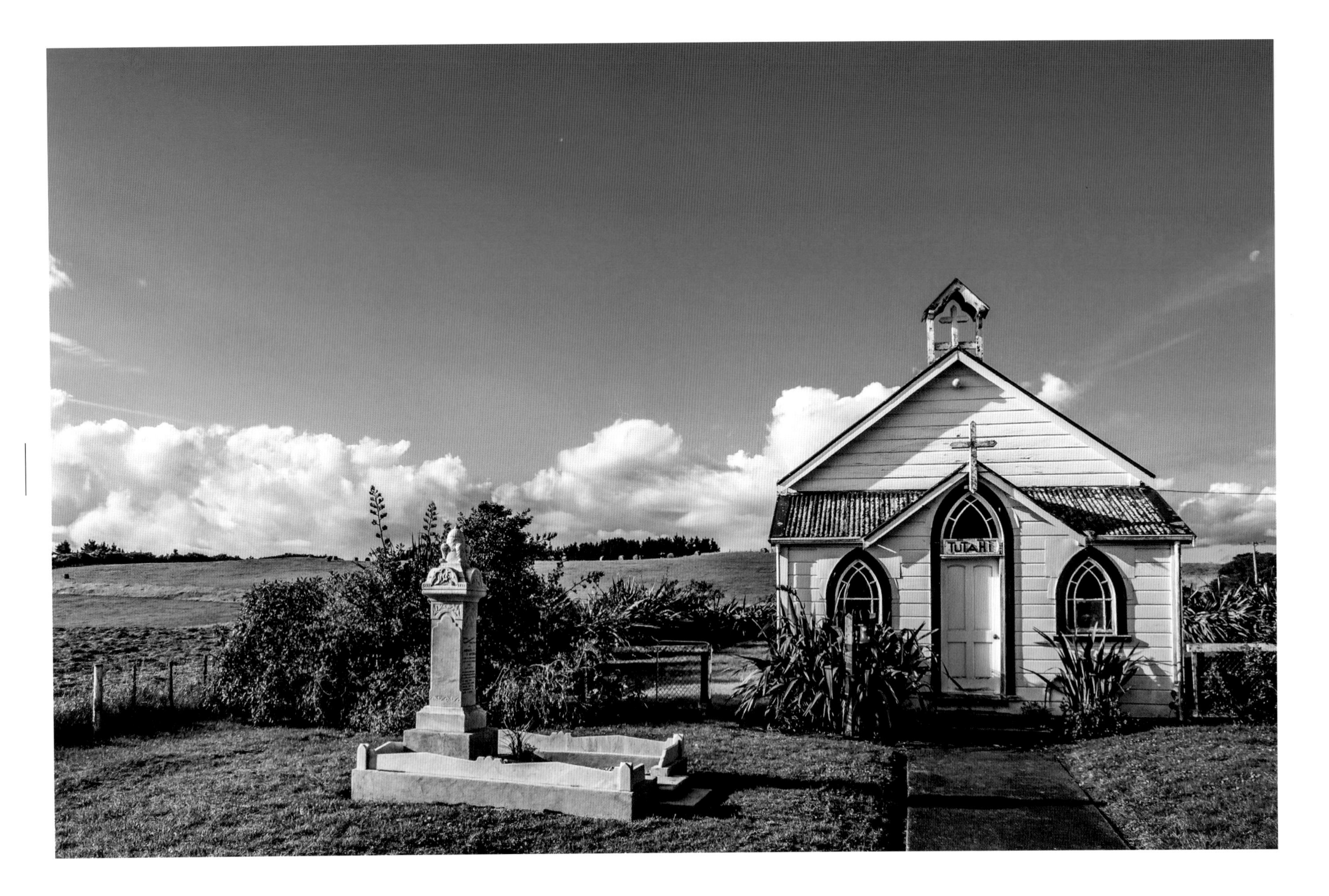

Resting Place

This small Maori resting place has a special spiritual feel about it. The people here were clearly loved. If you are travelling from Hawera this is on your left not far out of Wanganui.

Canon 7D, 15–85mm at f8 and 1/500sec. ISO 100.

Sunset at Kai Iwi Beach

The setting sun has left the beach and is turning a few wispy clouds a pale red colour. Here, on the Whanganui coast, the sand is a grey/black colour (in common with many west coast beaches) which contrasts with the white cliffs also dotted along this coastline.

Nikon D810, 24–120mm at f8 and 1/20 sec. ISO 400.

Balgownie Dairy Whanganui

On the road out toward the Whanganui seaside suburb of Castlecliff is the Balgownie Dairy. It is one of those iconic New Zealand dairies of which there seem to be many, usually on a suburban street corner or on a main street passing through. Open all hours and painted blue. Being surrounded by power poles certainly helps the atmosphere of the image.

Nikon D810, 24–120mm at f8.0 and 1/250 sec. ISO 64.

George's Dining Room

Not just a fish-n-chip shop, Georges Dining Room in Whanganui is right in the CBD and offers great food. But the decor, with the fan, old photos and hanging swordfish, is from another era.

Nikon D800, 24–120mm at f9.5 and 1/30 sec. ISO 1600.

Ladies Restrooms Whanganui

There was a time, in another era, when ladies restrooms were quite common.

Nikon D810, 24–120mm at f8 and 1/30 sec. ISO 200.

The Embassy Whanganui

The retro charm of the Embassy Theartre in Wanganui. Art deco colours and design.

Nikon D810, 24–120mm at f8 and 1/125 sec. ISO 200.

Royal Whanganui Opera House 1

A very wide angle lens captures the interior of the Opera House, with its amazing ceiling, ornate gold balcony, and red carpet coming down the aisles. Whanganui has a number of well preserved old buildings – this is one.

Nikon D810, Samyang 14mm at f9.5 and 8 seconds. ISO 64. On tripod.

Royal Whanganui Opera House 2

The gold pillars, and window reliefs, match the interior of the Opera House. Built in 1899 it has a splendour from an earlier time.

Nikon D810, 24–120mm at f9.5 and 1/45 sec. ISO 100.

RANGITIKEI/MANAWATU/HOROWHENUA **A Special Place Near Taihape**

Not far outside Taihape, set in the slightly rugged rolling farmland of the area, is this beautiful Maori church and cemetery.
What makes this place unique is that it seems to stand alone, lovingly cared for, amongst the rural hills and valleys that are all around Taihape.
Being in such a place creates a feeling of peace and solitude.
Nikon D750, 24–120mm at f9.5 and 1/350 sec. ISO 100.

Old Farmhouse Near Taihape

In the rolling country around Taihape this old farmhouse has long since had its power disconnected, and has reverted to being a shelter for the sheep.

Nikon D810, 24–120mm at f9.5 and 1/125 sec. ISO 64.

The Majestic Taihape

Still showing movies in Taihape, population 1700!

Nikon D810, 24–120mm at f8 and 1/125 sec. ISO 100.

Halcombe

I often look for 'iconic' small town New Zealand scenes and Halcombe, on the road between Fielding and Marton, is one. This image is helped by the dark clouds, and the fact that there is a pub on one side and a dairy on the other, with the Cenotaph in the middle of the town square.

Canon 7D, 15–85mm at f9.5 and 1/90 sec. ISO 100.

Foxton Clock

Foxton is one of those places where you don't realise there is a whole part of the town you don't see when driving down State Highway 1. Just half a kilometre toward the coast is Foxton town proper, with old shops, a great bakery – and of course the town clock. Being 'hung out' over the street makes the clock unique, and a bit hard to miss.

Nikon D5600, 18–55mm at f8 and 1/750 sec. ISO 100.

Farm Buildings Foxton

Old farm buildings with derelict trucks and machinery can often be found when driving around the New Zealand countryside. This one is just outside Foxton. It is early summer and there is still plenty of grass – blowing slightly in the wind.

Canon 7D, 15–85mm at f8 and 1/350 sec. ISO 100.

Fuel for the Engine – Palmerston North

Just off the Square in Palmerston North is the Burger Fuel restaurant. I could not resist stopping to take this picture. I did not have a tripod but luckily there was just enough light for a hand held shot.

Olympus OMD EM10, 9–18mm at f6.7 and 0.7 sec. ISO 800. Hand held.

Regent Theatre Pahiatua

Some small towns still have their picture theatre, and Pahiatua in the Tararua district is one such place. This movie theatre is community owned and operated, and still has the art-deco look from its heyday.

Canon 7D, 15–85mm at f8 and 1/125 sec. ISO 100.

Green Grey

You will see many of these farm water storage tanks as you travel around New Zealand. They are used to keep the water troughs full for stock, especially during summer. In this case it is winter – the grass is a deep green, and the dark clouds with a shaft of sunlight coming through create a quite different sort of image.

Canon 7D, 15–85mm at f8 and 1/500 sec. ISO 100.

Old Grandstand Masterton Showgrounds

In its heyday, at the annual A&P (Agricultural and Pastoral) Show, this grandstand would have been near full with farming folk and their families. The A&P Show is still an annual event with a combination of competitions for cattle, sheep and farm animals, and events like the 'gum boot toss' and the 'wine barrel roll' where locals show their skills. Pure Kiwiana.

Nikon D7200, 18–105mm at f8 and 1/750 sec. ISO 200.

Sunrise at Castle Point Lighthouse

This is one of those images where a bit of planning was required. Getting this shot necessitated a climb up and around to cliffs on the outside of the lagoon, high above the sea – in the pre-dawn light. Care was required – fishermen have lost their lives here. But it proves worth it, with the orange light just at sunrise shining directly onto the cliffs below the lighthouse.

Canon 7D, 15–85mm at f8 and 1/90 sec. ISO 100.

Castle Point Lagoon

Castle Point is one of the few settlements on the windswept Wairarapa coast. High up on the lagoon sea wall and looking south this is what you see. There is a rough beauty to the place, and the land and rock formations are truly special. The entrance to the lagoon can just be made out below the towering Castle Rock in the distance. One has to be careful scrabbling about here as a fall over the edge would have serious consequences.

Canon 7D, 15–85mm at f13 and 1/125 sec. ISO 100.

Choices – Masterton

On the main street of Masterton (State Highway 2) at the roundabout is a McDonalds on the left and a Burger King on the right, and just down the road a Subway.

Nikon D7200, 18–105mm at f6.7 and 1/8 sec. ISO 400. Handheld.

The Royal Oak Carterton

The Royal Oak Hotel stands on the main road through Carterton, in the Wairarapa.
Here you can have a beer, get a pub meal, place a bet on the horses or play the pokies, or get a room if you need one.

Nikon D7200, 18–105mm at f6.7 and 1/750 sec. ISO 100.

Old House Near Gladestone

Another old disused farm house, this time near Gladestone, in the Wairarapa.

Canon 600D, 18–55mm at f9.5 and 1/250 sec. ISO 100.

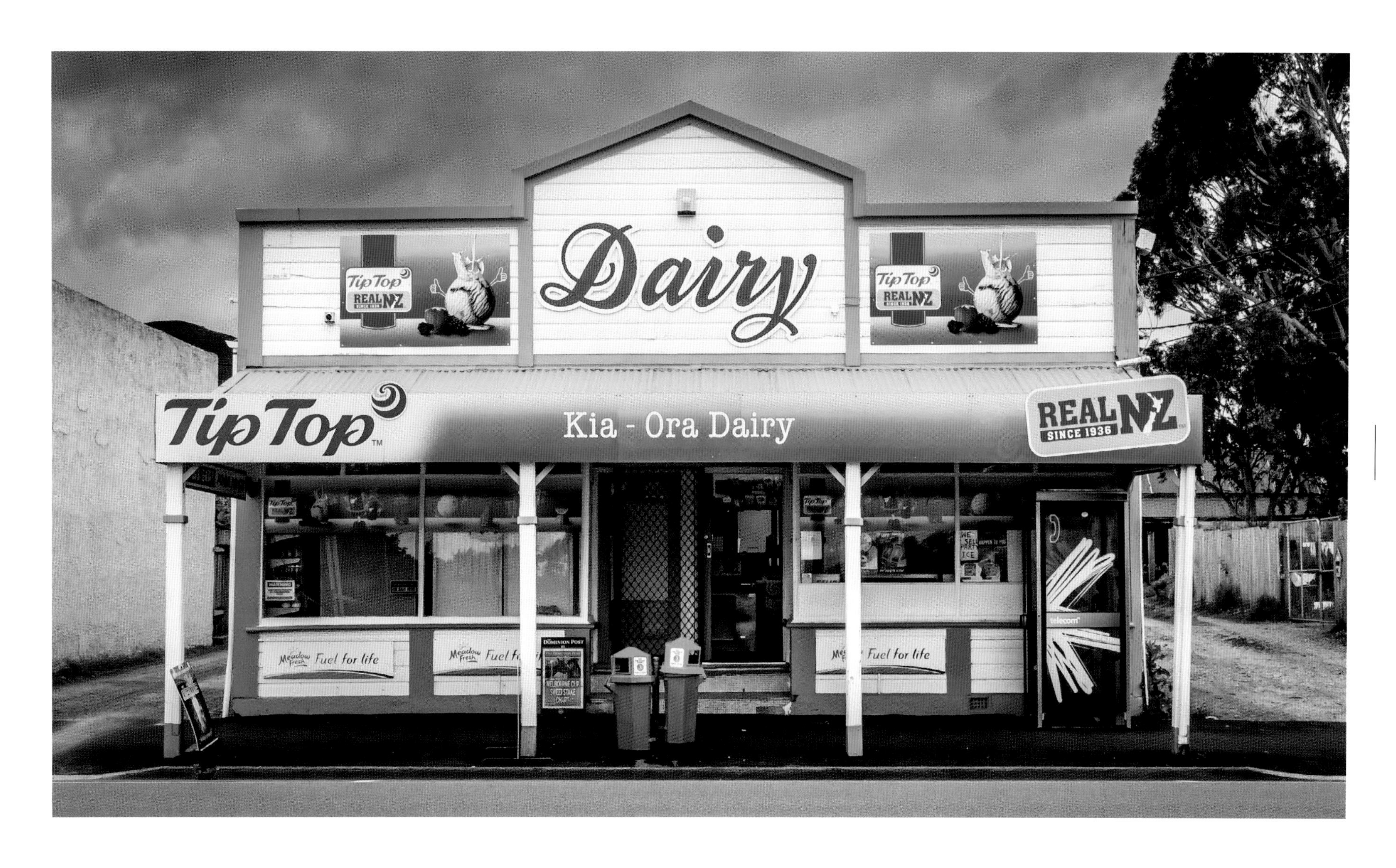

Kia Ora Dairy

All small towns and suburbs have their dairy but this one is special. It captures iconic New Zealand – sells Tip Top ice cream and is open all hours. Sadly this version of the Kia Ora Dairy, in blue and in Featherston, is no more.

Olympus XZ–1 at f5 and 1/400 sec. ISO 100.

Putangirua Pinnacles

The Putangirua Pinnacles are on the road to Ngawi on the Wairarapa south coast. This is a spectacular site but if it is a sunny day (as here) then you have to be there around the middle of the day, before the shadows cover the towering columns. This wide angle image gives a good idea of the majestic beauty of the place. It is a short, easy half hour walk up the dry stream bed to the base of the pinnacles.

Nikon D800, 24–85mm at f9.5 and 1/180 sec. ISO 100.

Cape Palliser

Cape Palliser is the southernmost part of the North Island. A dirt road leads past Ngawi and the lighthouse, and round the coast from there. This scene is taken late afternoon and captures the rich dry golden brown of the land, and the blue sky. The sun is directly behind to light up the landscape.

Canon 550D, 10–22mm at f16 and 1/90 sec. ISO 100.

Room with a View

Looking straight out to sea from the Wairarapa south coast, near Ngawi.

Canon 1000D, 18–55mm at f16 and 1/10 sec. ISO 200.

Kaitoke Revisited

WELLINGTON

I discovered this stream years ago when I purchased my first DSLR camera. The Kaitoke Regional Park is just north of Upper Hutt and was the venue for a number of *Lord of the Rings* scenes. This particular place is off the entry road, and can be hard to find. The profusion of moss covered rocks, hanging vines and ferns along the banks of the stream give you a feeling of being in the deepest New Zealand bush, but in reality you are barely half an hour from Wellington.

Nikon D800E, 24–120mm at f13 and 1 1/2 seconds. ISO 100. On tripod (VR off).

Eagar of Kerry – Karori Cemetery

Karori Cemetry in Wellington has many old gravestones and monuments, and family tombs. Here is one.

Nikon D7200, 18–105mm at f9.5 and 1/45 sec. ISO 100.

Near Civic Square

Te Aho a Maui in Civic Square, Wellington, represents the Maori myth whereby Maui fishes up the North Island from the sea. You can walk through the 'split pyramid' to the Sea Bridge on the other side. On this day the storm clouds hang over Maui and the city.

Olympus OMD EM10, 14–42mm at f6.7 and 1/45 sec. ISO 200. Processed into Dramatic Tone.

Queen Victoria

In Kent Terrace, Wellington, this statue of Queen Victoria sits amid the rushing traffic. She is holding her sceptre in her right hand and a globe with an angel shining the light, in her left hand. The detail is to behold.

Canon 7D, 15–85mm at f6.7 and 1/60 sec. ISO 200.

Burgers are King

I could not resist – there was only one other person in the restaurant. The reds and whites of the tables, with shiny red seats, just begged to be photographed.

Olympus OMD EM5 II, 14–42mm at f8 and 1/6 sec. ISO 200. Handheld. (It pays to always carry your camera with you.)

Camel Grill

The Camel Grill sits just on the edge of Pigeon Park in central Wellington. The area is usually thronging with people and it took some patient timing to get this shot, with just the owner having a quick break.

Olympus OM–D EM5, 14–42mm at f9.5 and 1/90 sec. ISO 200. Processed into 'Dramatic Tone'.

Day of the Dead

A little alleyway just off Cuba Street in Wellington commemorates the Mexican Day of the Dead, when family members and friends who have died are remembered. The 'Day of the Little Angels' is often the day before – in memory of children who have died. The imagery is unusual and may, they say, come from Aztec origins.

Olympus OMD EM10, 14–42mm at f8 and 1/6 sec. ISO 800. Handheld.

Gone Fishing

In the days before mobile phones there were phone boxes – even when you went fishing. A quiet spot looking across the entrance to Wellington Harbour.

Olympus XZ–1 at f4 and 1/125 sec. ISO 100.

Point Halswell Wellington

In Wellington you can drive all the way round the shoreline and bays from the central city to the south coast. This small lighthouse is on the point where the ferries turn toward the docking terminal.

Canon 550D, 18–55mm at f11 and 1/90 sec. ISO 100.

Point Dorset Wellington

The Wellington south coast is a windswept, rugged and spectacular coastline – all within minutes of the city itself. But on a good day (as any Wellingtonian will tell you) it has a beauty all of its own. Point Dorset is at the eastern end of the south coast, near the entrance to Wellington Harbour. Late in the day the sun is shining on the jagged rocks and on the Pencarrow Head lighthouse in the far distance. An invigorating place to be.

Nikon D7200, 18–105mm at f8 and 1/45 sec. ISO 100.

Platinum Nails – Wellington

It is the end of the day and Platinum Nails is ready for tomorrow's customers.

Olympus OMD EM5 II, 9–18mm at f8 and 1/30 sec. ISO 200.

Zebra Backpackers – Wellington

Do you remember, before camper vans and freedom camping, when backpackers were the common tourist visitor? There are still some, and here is where they can stay in Wellington. You certainly can't park your camper van overnight this close to the CBD.

Olympus OMD EM5, 14–42mm at f6.7 and 1/250 sec. ISO 200.

Pop-In Candy Store

In Kilbirnie, Wellington, a corner dairy with a difference. Designed to catch the kids on the way to school?

Nikon D5200, 18–55mm at f8 and 1/1000 sec. ISO 100.

Scrap

Her face on the wrecked bus, and her statement about 'reliability' and 'commitment' just hit me. The scrap yard is near Porirua, Wellington.

Canon 1000D, 18–55mm at f9.5 and 1/125 sec. ISO 100.

Insurance Policy

Another one of those city images I could not resist – although I had to come back several times to avoid parked cars. This is in Porirua, Wellington. I thought there was a (slight) irony in these places being side by side, but maybe there isn't?

Nikon D7200, Sigma 10–20mm at f8 and 1/60 sec. ISO 100.

Wellington South Coast

This long exposure captures the movement of the waves around the rough rocks of the Wellington south coast.

Nikon D800E, 24–85mm at f11 and 15 seconds. ISO 100. ND filter plus tripod, with VR off.

Totaranui Beach

The golden beaches along the northern boundary of Abel Tasman National Park are very well known, and popular. There is a large camping ground at Totaranui, but outside of summer it is essentially empty. Here at the western end of the beach a cloudy day seems to give the sand and rock formations a deeper colour. A short walk from here will take you round the coast to Anapai Bay – also a beautiful place, and only accessible by boat or walking track.

Nikon D800, 24–120mm at f16 and 1/60 sec. ISO 100.

Takaka River

This small, still inlet off the Takaka River is located in the Payne's Ford Reserve, and is found after an easy walk along the track by the river. The limestone rock formations are all around this area. The dull overcast day makes the place seem gloomy and mellow.

Nikon D800, 24–120mm at f16 and 1/4 second. ISO 100. On tripod (VR off).

Beach at Rabbit Island

Low cloud and low tide at Rabbit Island beach, near Nelson. On a day like this the long flat beach seems like an open expanse that may never end.

Nikon D7200, 18–105mm at f8 and 1/750 sec. ISO 200.

Shipwreck Motueka Mudflats

The mudflats lie only a couple of kilometres from Motueka township itself, and a short walk along the shoreline will bring you to this old wreck. There is something about an old wreck sitting alone on the shore, especially on a dismal grey day – the black and white image accentuates this feeling.

Nikon D7200, 18–105mm at f8 and 1/60 sec. ISO 100.

Old House Near Motueka

The symmetry of the house and tree in the ploughed paddock caught my eye, and I turned around to go back and capture it.

Canon 550D, 18–55mm at f9.5 and 1/250 sec. ISO 100.

Moria Gate Arch – Oparara

Located in the Oparara Basin just north of Karamea on the West Coast the Moria Gate Arch is one of the most beautiful limestone arches in the country. A shingle road provides access and is narrow in places (don't take a large camper van) but it is an easy, short walk to the arch. It is possible to walk under the arch by clambering down through a small cave entrance. Late in the day is the best time as most visitors have departed.

Nikon D7200, 18–105mm at f11 and 1/15 sec. ISO 200.

Cut'n Edge Westport

The beautiful colours and the style of the building captured me. Clearly the building is from an earlier time, but has been beautifully painted. I think I can make out, in the central lettering below the spire, the letters 'UFS' – so a UFS Dispensary in past days?

Canon 550D, 18–55mm at f5.6 and 1/20 sec. ISO 100.

To Accommodate – Westport

On the road out of Westport, on the way to Karamea, you will come across this 'art hotel'.
A gallery and accommodation in case you had not noticed. The sentiments in the words are definitely telling us something.

Nikon D810, 24–120mm at f8 and 1/180 sec. ISO 100.

Old Workers Union Hall Runanga

'United We Stand'. There is just enough peeling paint left on this old weathered building to tell us that the Miners Hall was opened in 1908. In those days Runanga would have been a thriving mining town. If you look carefully you can see that this is now the community hall for the town.

Nikon D800E, 24–85mm at f11 and 1/45 sec. ISO 100.

Cape Foulwind Revisited 1

I have been to Cape Foulwind near Westport a number of times. In this image the even light of an overcast day has allowed the camera to capture the subtle colours, shadows and shapes of the rocks around the sea cliffs. Getting down to the beach is achieved from Highway 67A running along the northern edge of the shoreline. Even at low tide one has to be prepared to get wet feet in order to navigate around some of the cliffs.

Nikon D7200, 18–105mm at f11 and 1/20 sec. ISO 100.

Cape Foulwind Revisited 2

Cape Foulwind, near Westport, is a photographer's delight, especially on an overcast, cloudy day. The mottled grey cliffs come down almost vertically into the sand and, as you can see, have a spectacular beauty. If you get there on a weekday (at low tide) you will have this amazing place to yourself.

Nikon D7200, 18–105mm at f11 and 1/60 sec. ISO 100.

Storm Gathers over Woodpecker Bay

Woodpecker Bay is a few kilometres north of Punakaiki on the West Coast of the South Island. At the southern end of the beach where this shot was taken there are a series of rocky outcrops. The rock in the image is just where the beach starts to merge with the rocks. This place has a bleak exposed beauty on a winters day.

Nikon D800E, 24–85mm at f13 and 1/60 sec. ISO 100.

In Paparoa National Park

Bullock Creek Road near Punakaiki will take you several kilometres in to the Paparoa National Park. High limestone cliffs are common in this area and off the road the bush can be almost impenetrable, with steep climbs and descents. This wide angle image was taken hand held as there was no stable placement for a tripod, and luckily one shot came out sharp. The mossy ferns cover the tree trunks.

Canon EOS M3, 11–22mm at f9 and 1/3rd sec. ISO 200. (Handheld with good image stabilised lens.)

Truman Beach

The Truman Track is just 3 km north of Punakaiki on the West Coast. It is a short easy walk down to the beach and is best seen at low tide; and early in the morning before the tourists have arrived. The rock formations carved out by the sea stand in clear relief against the pristine smooth sand.

Nikon D810, 24–120mm at f16 and 1/45 sec. ISO 100.

Motukiekie Rocks

There are many unique West Coast places that can only be reached at low tide – and this is another of them. The Motukiekie Rocks are situated at 12 Mile Bluff just north of Greymouth. The low tide window is really no more than an hour – before one is in danger of getting trapped by the incoming tide. There are actually six rock outcrops just out from the low tide mark, but in this image it looks like four. Apart from the possibility of meeting one or two locals you will have the place to yourself.

Nikon D810, 24–120mm at f16 and 1/30 sec. ISO 64.

Lake Wahapo Mist

There is a prehistoric, medieval feel to parts of the south Westland swamp forest. Here the early morning mist at the northern end of Lake Wahapo slowly swirls around the tree roots and flax bushes at the lake edge.

Nikon D800E, 24–85mm at f9.5 and 1/1000 sec. ISO 100.

Sunrise at Lake Mapourika – South Westland

Getting up early has its rewards – the lake is perfectly still and the mist is just starting to lift. A bit of scrabbling along the shore finds this old log with bits and pieces growing out of it.

Nikon D810, 24–120mm at f13 and 1/30 sec. ISO 64.

Dawn Mist – Lake Mapourika

It is early morning on Lake Mapourika just north of Franz Joseph. It is perfectly still and quiet. No-one else is around. The sun has yet to emerge through the mist.

Nikon D810, 24–120mm at f11 and 1/10 sec. ISO 100. Handheld.

Southern Alps from Lake Matheson

This is one of those beautiful and iconic places on the West Coast. The easy walking track takes you right round the small lake, with several viewing spots as you go. The trick in an image like this is to be patient, wait for the breeze to drop and the lake surface to go perfectly smooth – in this case the wait was only one hour.

Nikon D800, 24–120mm at f8 and 1/250 sec. ISO 100.

End of Day

Dawn and dusk are the photographer's best times of the day. The sun is low and lights up the scene with shadows and highlights not seen at other times of day. Here is an example – taken from the eastern end of the walk around Lake Matheson, near Fox Glacier on the West Coast.

Nikon D800, 24–120mm at f8 and 1/80 sec. ISO 100.

Out of the Mist

I was at Lake Paringa, South Westland, in the early morning intending the catch the autumn mist. As I am watching, a kayaker slowly glides out of the mist, paddle across his kayak.

Nikon D800E, 24–85mm at f9.5 and 1/1000 sec. ISO 100.

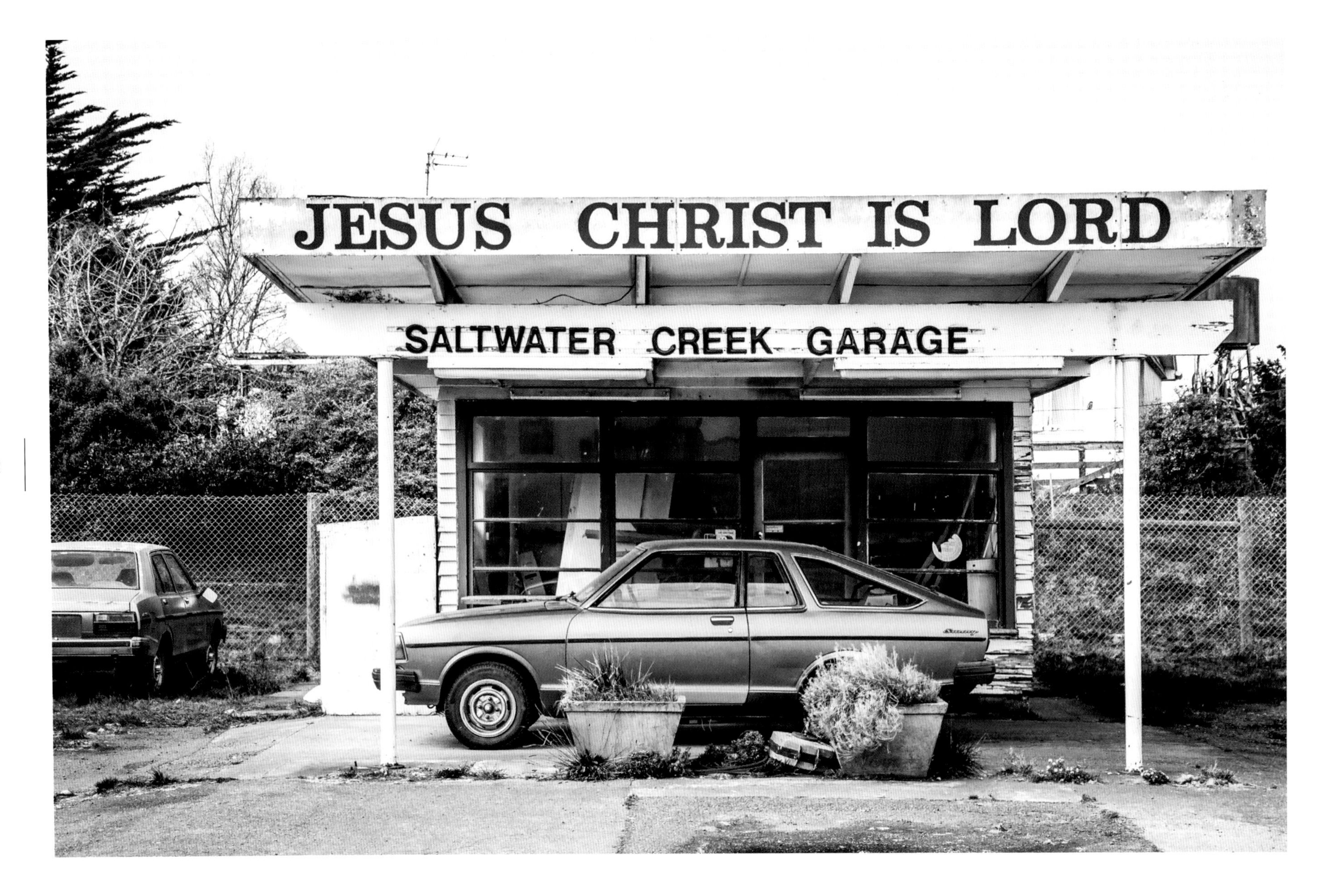

CANTERBURY

Jesus is Lord

Taken somewhere near Amberley just north of Christchurch. An old garage/service station with a message. The early model Datsun cars just seem to add to the image.

Canon 7D, 15–85mm at f8 and 1/125 sec. ISO 100.

Castle Hill Mono

The rock formations at Castle Hill on the road through Arthurs Pass are famous. For a landscape photographer the challenge is to capture a unique perspective. This black and white image necessitated walking round to the rear of the formations (not a long walk) and searching for a scene that captured the scale and the range of unusual shapes. It also helped to pick a time and day when not too many people were about.

Nikon D7200, 18–105mm at f9.5 and 1/350 sec. ISO100.

Sunrise at Lake Pearson

It is autumn at Lake Pearson, on the road to Arthurs Pass and the West Coast. The early morning mist is starting to lift. Just a few minutes walk along the shoreline from the parking area brings you to this beautiful scene.

Nikon D810, 24–120mm at f8 and 1/125 sec. ISO 64.

Toward Torlesse Range

Late in the day, just off the road from Arthurs Pass to Christchurch, near Castle Hill. The Torlesse Range is in the distance.

Canon 550D, 18–55mm at f16 and 1/45 sec. ISO 100.

Arcadia Theatre Waimate

Many small towns around New Zealand used to have their own picture theatre. Here is the old Arcadia Theatre from Waimate in South Canterbury. Now largely empty it seems a somewhat forlorn reminder of small town life back in the 40s and 50s.

Canon 7D, 15–85mm at f8 and 1/45 sec. ISO 100.

Tasman Glacier Lake McKENZIE COUNTRY/SOUTHERN ALPS

When you get to Mt Cook Village (the Hermitage) you can end up with two simple choices for walking and exploring – left toward the Hooker Valley or right toward the Tasman Valley. This image is from the moraine above the Tasman Glacier lake. If you look carefully the glacier terminal can be seen at the far end. The perfectly smooth and even grey of the lake water makes this scene.

Nikon D800, 24–120mm at f16 and 1/45 sec. ISO 100.

Lake Alexandrina in Winter

Truly a special place. Lake Alexandrina, near Tekapo, is a small lake with cribs (baches) at the southern end where this shot was taken. The holiday season has long passed and we are in to winter. There is not a soul around. The deep blues of the sky are reflected in the lake as you look toward Hall Range and the Southern Alps.

Nikon D800, 24–120mm at f11 and 1/125 sec. ISO 100.

Lake Tekapo at Dawn

Lake Tekapo is a very popular tourist stop but if you get up early you can still catch the tranquil beauty of a still lake at dawn. This shot was taken at the shoreline just below the Church of the Good Shepherd. In the background at the end of the lake is Observation Hill with Mt Erebus to the left.

Nikon D7200, 18–105mm at f9.5 and 1/15 sec. ISO 100.

Lake Tekapo Lupins

Walking along the Lake Tekapo foreshore when the lupins are in flower is not to be missed. Although they are technically classed as a weed the lupins have become a bit of a tourist attraction. I have to admit to having had them on my list of places to visit for quite a while. Late November is the time to catch them. As you walk along the scented smell wafts through the air, and the vivid colours are all around you.

Nikon D7200, 18–105mm at f13 and 1/125 sec. ISO 200.

Aorangi /Mt Cook from Tasman River Flats

The Tasman River flats start just north of Glentanner on the road to the Hermitage and Aorangi/Mt Cook. At sunrise in the middle of winter the frost is still on the ground, and the water lying around is ice. There is not one cloud in the sky, and the mountain can be seen in perfect clarity. At this time of the day all is quiet apart from the odd bird call. Magic!

Nikon D800, 24–120mm at f11 and 1/125 sec. ISO 100.

Storm Clouds Over Lake Pukaki

I have photographed beautiful Lake Pukaki before but not with dark storm clouds over the lake. I was lucky to get this image, given the weather was not ideal and the wind was starting to blow across the lake. The pattern of the clouds reflected in the still waters makes for a gloomy feel. Aoraki/Mt Cook is almost completely hidden in the distance.

Nikon D810, 24–120mm at f16 and 1/125 sec. ISO 64.

Ben Ohau Range

Lake Pukaki is perfectly still. The sun has set behind the Ben Ohau Range. As the colours fade in the dusk there is still enough light in the sky to create a beautiful reflection.

Nikon D800, 24–120mm at f 13 and 1/30 sec. ISO 100.

Telegraph Poles McKenzie Country

The telegraph poles seem to capture the vast open spaces of the McKenzie Country. If you look closely the poles appear to stretch on forever. There is a hazy, fine mist hiding the hills and mountains in the distance.

Nikon D800, 24–120mm at f8 and 1/60 sec. ISO 100.

Lake Ohau Toward the Alps

Looking down Lake Ohau late on a sunny afternoon. Mt Glen Lyon and Mt Glenmary are dead centre at the end of the lake, with the Southern Alps proper behind. Off to the right is the Ben Ohau Range. The very slight ripple in the lake waters is making the reflected clouds shimmer.

Canon 550D, 18–55mm at f11 and 1/125 sec. ISO 100.

Toward Mt Ohau

There are many beautiful places in the MacKenzie Country – lakes and mountains and open spaces.
The simplicity of this image, taken late in the day, with Mt Ohau in the background, captures something of the MacKenzie.

Nikon D810, 24–120mm at f16 and 1/30 sec. ISO 64.

Clay Cliffs Revisited

The Omarama Clay Cliffs in the MacKenzie Country are a spectacular example of glacial erosion, with towering columns and pinnacles. On a sunny day the sunlight casts shadows over one side of the canyon bringing these pillars and ravines into sharp relief. A short drive up a private shingle road (with $5 entrance fee) is required.

Nikon D810, 24–120mm at f11 and 1/90 sec. ISO 64

Ahuriri Valley

The Ahuriri Valley is a sparsely populated but not too remote place accessed by shingle road a few kilometres north of Lindis Pass. It has that wonderful peace that comes from being in a vast, open, empty place (although you may see the occasional fisherman).

Nikon D800, 24–120mm at f13 and 1/90 sec. ISO 100.

Lake Benmore

If you climb the hill near the parking area by Benmore dam itself you eventually come to this small ridge looking due north. Lake Benmore is below and in the far distance (almost visible) is Lake Pukaki and the Southern Alps.

Canon 550D, 18–55mm at f 16 and 1/20 sec. ISO 100.

Benmore Toilets

There are public toilets scattered all over New Zealand, in towns and even in many small localities. On the road to the Benmore Dam you will come across the Benmore public toilets. For some quaint reason these have a distinctly Egyptian or Mediterranean style to them. The water tank on top has Egyptian figures painted on it.

Canon 550D, 18–55mm at f9.5 and 1/500 sec. ISO 100.

Lindis Hills Early Morning

There are many beautiful and majestic places in New Zealand that are easily accessible, often requiring only a very short walk from the car. This is one of them. Just park the car near the summit of the pass, on the north side, but get there early on a clear day. The hills around Lindis Pass are convoluted and run together down into the valley below. The early dawn sun creates the shadows and light that make the hills so impressive.

Nikon D800, 24–120mm at f4 and 1/500 sec. ISO 100.

Steampunk HQ Oamaru

Oamaru has a vibrant 'old quarter' just off the CBD. Here steampunk culture, with its combination of Victorian age steam and retro-sci fi, is alive and well. Weird futuristic steam trains and machinery abound – a sort of dystopian celebration.

Canon 7D, 15–85mm at f8 and 1/125 sec. ISO 100.

Tiger Tea

There was a time when people drank more tea than coffee, and Tiger Tea was one of the most popular. I was taken not only by the 'Tiger Tea' sign but also the old prams outside the store. Hampden is one of those small settlements on State Highway 1 between Oamaru and Dunedin.

Nikon D810, 24–120mm at f9.5 and 1/250 sec. ISO 100.

Old Pier St Clair Beach

Dunedin has beautiful, often windswept beaches. St Clair beach merges into St Kilda Beach, and this old pier is down the St Clair end. A long exposure late in the day gives the sea a smooth milky look.

Canon 7D, 15–85mm at f11 and 15 seconds. ISO 100. On tripod.

The Last Video Store

This may not be the 'last video store' but it could be. Once prolific around New Zealand there are only one or two left and this one is in South Dunedin. There is something sad about the passing of a technology, and an era when one went to the video store to browse the racks and find the nights entertainment.

Nikon D810, 24–120mm at f8 and 1/250 sec. ISO 100.

Tunnel Beach

A visit to Tunnel Beach south of Dunedin is a treat for any photographer or nature lover. The small beach is entered through a tunnel, and the cliffs are close, towering above you. Just pick a time close to low tide otherwise you will get wet!

Canon 550D, 18–55mm at f5.6 and 1/250 sec. ISO 100.

Danseys Pass

Getting to Danseys Pass involves taking the road from Naseby to Duntroon, a shingle road in good condition. To get this shot I stopped at the pass itself and climbed up the eastern slope toward the schist rocks – no more than a kilometre – and waited for the late afternoon sun. Lower Ben Lomond is in the centre of the frame.

Nikon D810, 24–120mm at f13 and 1/90 sec. ISO 64.

Hawkduns Winter 1

It is winter and the snow has arrived in the Maniatoto, completely covering the Hawkdun Range. It is a cold overcast day, but completely still.

Nikon D800, 24–120mm at f9.5 and 1/125 sec. ISO 100.

Hawkduns Winter 2

A cold, bleak beauty near the Hawkdun Range. The old farm buildings are deserted. Tussock pokes up through the snow. The wind has dropped and a grey, slightly misty stillness seems to pervade the place.

Nikon D800, 24–120mm at f5.6 and 1/350 sec. ISO 100.

Hawkduns Winter 3

In winter this long straight range is capped with snow and makes a spectacular boundary to the Maniatoto plains, stretching from Naseby, past St Bathans toward Omarama. On a still, clear day the sky seems vast.

Nikon D800, 24–120mm at f8 and 1/350 sec. ISO 100.

Falls Dam Early Morning

Falls Dam sits in the back country of the Maniatoto near St Bathans, and is accessible via shingle road and ideally a 4WD vehicle. Looking across the lake behind the dam the Hawkdun Range is on the right and Mt St Bathans is in the distance on the left. In this dawn shot the air is still and cold, and winter snow will soon cover the Hawkduns.

Canon 550D, 18–55mm at f13 and 1/45 sec. ISO 200.

Blue Lake in Winter

Here the Blue Lake is truly blue. The lake is artificial, having its origins in gold mining operations (sluicing or water blasting) around 100 years ago.
The mineral enriched water gives the lake a blue appearance, aided by the clear blue skies so common in Central Otago.
On a still day, with a mirror like surface, this is what you see.

Nikon D800, 24–120mm at f16 and 1/60 sec. ISO 100.

Blue Lake on Grey Day

The Blue Lake at St Bathans in Central Otago is a well known photographic destination. But on this day the moody dark clouds over the lake are reflected in the perfectly still surface and make for a quite different feel.

Nikon D800E, 24–85mm at f8.0 and 1/500 sec. ISO 100.

Maniatoto Dawn

The Maniatoto in Central Otago can get very cold in winter. Dawn often brings a mist or fog which soon clears when the sun comes up, as is happening in this image. Looking down the long straight roads of the Maniatoto brings a sense of vastness – of sky and land.

Canon 550D, 18–55mm at f8 and 1/90 sec. ISO 100.

Cloudy Day at Poolburn Reservoir

In the dry barren country behind Alexandra lies the Poolburn Reservoir. It's cold in winter and hot in summer. There are a few holiday baches (cribs to South Islanders) scattered about but on this winter's day the place is desolate, cold and empty.

Canon 550D, 18–55mm at f16 and 1/45 sec. ISO 100.

Hunter's Cabin

Clearly the bus was towed to this desolate area in Central Otago – but from where I do not know. It would be very cold in winter.

Canon 550D, 18–55mm at f16 and 1/30 sec. ISO 100.

Special Place at Poolburn Reservoir

The Poolburn Reservior is located in the barren semi desert of the high country behind Alexandra in Central Otago.
Hot in summer and cold in winter, the 'special place' is not insulated.

Canon 550D, 18–55mm at f16 and 1/60 sec. ISO 100.

Fishing Hut Lake Onslow

There are a few fishing huts scattered around Lake Onslow, in the high plateau country behind Roxburgh and Millers Flat.
It is a place that is both beautiful and desolate at the same time – lovely on a still day in summer but bitterly cold and often covered with snow in winter.
There are shingle roads or tracks right through here and on to Patearoa in the Maniatoto.

Nikon D810, 24–120mm at f16 and 1/60 sec. ISO 64.

Toward Lammerlaw Range

This scene is captured from the top of the Lammermoor Range near Ailsa Craig, looking west toward the Lammerlaws and Knobby Range. This area is an extensive, open plateau in the hinterland between Middlemarch and Alexandra. The shingle road into Te Papanui Conservation Park is drivable but eventually peters out into boggy tracks – especially in winter!

Canon 550D, 50–250mm at f9.5 and 1/350 sec. ISO 100.

Lammerlaw Range

The Lammerlaws are part of the remote Central Otago high country between Alexandra and Middlemarch, reached by shingle road and not very accessible in winter. This is a musterer's hut near the high point of Ailsa Craig – it looks pleasant enough on this day but in winter the tussocks can be snow and sleet driven. There is a splendid isolation and unforgiving beauty all the same.

Canon 550D, 18–55mm at f16 and 1/60 sec. ISO 100.

Toward Mt Teviot

The road in to Lake Onslow from Millers Flat in Central Otago takes you past Mt Teviot – not so much a mountain as the high point before you head down to the lake. This shot captures the sun on the ridgeline in the distance, with cloud over the pine forest. Although it might not seem mountainous one is almost 900m up and it can get very cold in winter.

Nikon D810, 24–120mm at f8 and 1/90 sec. ISO 100.

Looking Toward Knobby Range 1

The folded hills of the Central Otago high country are captured in this image, taken from Mt Teviot and looking toward the Knobby Range. Late in the day the shadows create a pattern of tussock valleys and ridges.

Nikon D810, 24–120mm at f6.7 and 1/250 sec. ISO 100. (At 120mm the camera is planted carefully on a fencepost to ensure a sharp shot.)

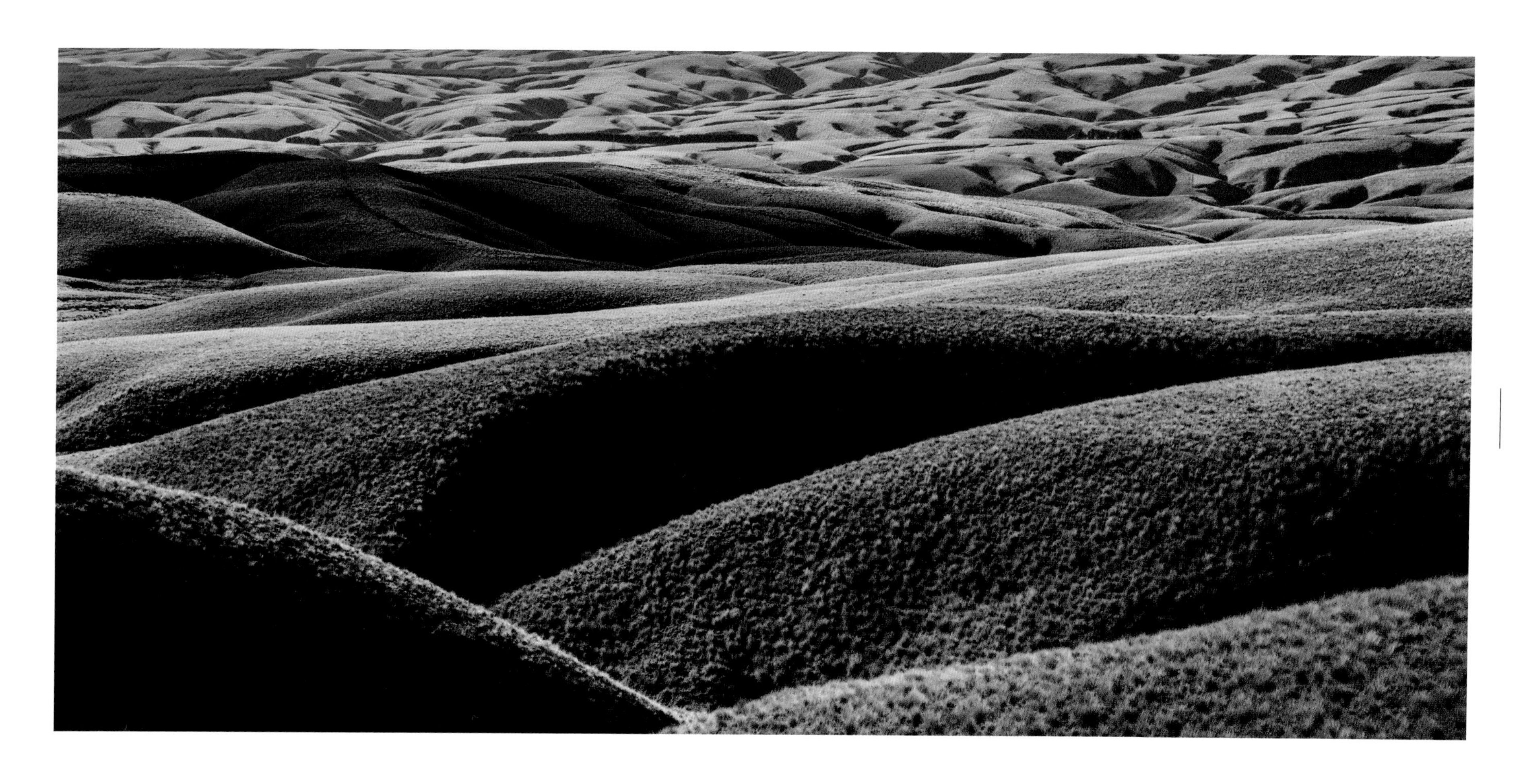

Looking Toward Knobby Range 2

On the road to Mt Teviot and Lake Onslow in Central Otago one gets up fairly high and can look across to the Knobby Range in the west. This shot is taken late in the day when the low sun is causing the valleys to fall into shadow. It is empty country and the convoluted hills and valleys provide a sort of pattern to the landscape.

Nikon D810, 24–120mm at f8 and 1/180 sec. ISO 64.

Alexandra Autumn

Colour and spindly shapes. These large old trees in a local Alexandra orchard capture autumn in Central Otago.

Canon 550D, 18–55mm at f13 and 1/15 sec. ISO 100. Handheld.

Old Man Range

Behind the town of Alexandra in Central Otago looms the Old Man Range. There are many schist rock outcrops along the range as it runs from Roxburgh to Cromwell – the trick is to find the right spot early in the morning, when the sun first shines on to the hills. In this case a solid walk up on to the range from Oreo Creek Road leads to an amazing variety of rocky ridges and views over the surrounding countryside – a stark beauty and splendid isolation. Just pick a fine day as it can get windswept and cold very quickly.

Nikon D800E, 24–120mm at f13.0 and 1/30 sec. ISO 100.

Butchers Dam in Winter 1

Just outside Alexandra on the road to Roxburgh one passes Butchers Dam. This is a winter shot and, as is often the case, the lake behind the dam is almost mirror smooth reflecting the schist rocks and surrounding hills.

Nikon D800E, 24–85mm at f11 and 1/30 sec. ISO 100.

Butchers Dam In Winter 2

Almost sunset at Butchers Dam near Alexandra in Central Otago. It is cold and completely still. The last rays of the sun are catching the shore line of the lake behind the dam. Snow can be seen on the Old Man Range in the far background.

Nikon D800, 24–120mm at f16 and 1/8 sec. ISO 100.

Bannockburn Sluicings

There is a fascinating history to the Bannockburn Sluicings. These are New Zealand's 'badlands' of the wild west. They are manmade – by the gold miners of the mid/late 1800s using large high powered water cannons to blast away the hills in search of gold. What is left is this barren but beautiful wasteland surrounded by cliffs. To get the full impact of this place you have to walk through the canyons close up, and ideally off the track.

Nikon D810, 24–120mm at f16 and 1/30 sec. ISO 64.

Administration Building Milton SOUTH OTAGO/SOUTHLAND

Milton in South Otago once had a thriving woollen mill. This old brick building was the administration office for the mill. It is from a grander time when this part of the town would have been a hive of activity based around the operations of the mill. Now the old admin building and parts of the old mill are used by local small businesses and community groups. A sign of the times in many small towns.

Canon 7D, 15–85mm at f8 and 1/90 sec. ISO 100.

Near Lawrence

The late afternoon sun casts shadows over farmland just south of Lawrence in South Otago.

Canon 7D, 15–85mm at f8 and 1/250 sec. ISO 200.

At Kaka Point

Kaka Point is on the coast between Balclutha and Owaka in South Otago. It is a popular place to have a bach (or a 'crib' as they call them down south) but in this case the crib does not appear to have been big enough. It faces directly onto the beach with amazing sea views – although I imagine it is cold and windswept in winter.

Nikon D800, 24–120mm at f8 and 1/250 sec. ISO 100.

McLean Falls Catlins

One of New Zealand's most beautiful waterfalls, with moss covered terraces and an easy track for access. There are really two waterfalls here – the upper one and the lower terraces. The falls are in the Catlins Conservation Park not far from the main road. If it has been raining, as was the case here, just be careful not to slip.

Nikon D810, 24–120mm at f16 and 4 seconds. ISO 64. On tripod (VR off).

Near McLean Falls

McLean Falls are just upstream from this spot but in a way these rocks, with the moss and grasses growing on them, seemed just as beautiful. There was some difficulty getting a stable place to set up my tripod (the exposure is 15 seconds long) but in the end it worked out, without the photographer falling into the stream.

Nikon D810, 24–120mm at f16 and 15 seconds. ISO 100. On tripod (VR off).

Stainless Steel

Another fairly common sight around rural New Zealand – this is the Edendale (Fonterra) dairy factory in Southland, between Gore and Invercargill. The huge stainless steel tanks shine in the afternoon sun. It looks conspicuously clean.

Nikon D800, 24–120mm at f8 and 1/350 sec. ISO 100.

Wanaka Tree in Mist FIORDLAND/LAKES DISTRICT

This special tree (its shape and place) sits on the edge of Lake Wanaka just near the foreshore walk. I had been waiting for a long time to capture the tree on a misty day, so that all one saw was the tree receding into the infinity of the mist.

Nikon D800, 24–120mm at f5.6 and 1/180 sec. ISO 100.

Milford Sound

Another of those beautiful places that are so easy to get to. But you must arrive before the tourists in their buses! This works well anyway as the early morning is easily the best time, with the mist swirling around those majestic peaks as they rise up out of the fiord. Make sure to also carry your sandfly repellent.

Nikon D800, 24–120mm at f16 and 1/60 sec. ISO 100.

Lake Marian

A short way down the Hollyford Valley Road the track up to Lake Marian begins. It is a steep rocky track for the most part, but has some glorious merits – first you go past Lake Marian Falls not far up the track and then, after some 2–3 hours, you arrive at this most beautiful 'hanging' lake suspended between mountain ranges. Pick a good weather day to go or you will not see much.

Nikon D800E, Samyang 14mm at f8.0 and 1/125 sec. ISO 100.

Dart River Valley

North of Glenorchy are the Dart and Rees valleys, and the start of the Routeburn Track. It is a beautiful area. A sealed road leads to the bridge over the Dart River so it is easily accessible. In this early morning shot a small reflection of the Southern Alps is caught in the still side waters of the river. I had to climb under the bridge and get down to river level for this image.

Nikon D800, 24–120mm at f16 and 1/30 sec. ISO 100.

Glenorchy Lagoon at Dawn

The Glenorchy Lagoon is an easy circular walk located just minutes from the shops and pub. At dawn or dusk, especially if it is still, it is a beautiful peaceful place with the mountains in the distance and the sky reflected on the waters of the lagoon.

Nikon D810, 24–120mm at f9.5 and 1/8 sec. ISO 64. On tripod.

Autumn Forest Arrowtown

Walking along the Arrowtown river bank at this time of year is something to remember. The orange/yellow autumn leaves are falling but still plentiful on the trees. The overcast day provides a subtle, even light through the whole scene, accentuating the fine patterns of the leaves and branches.

Nikon D800E, 24–85mm at f13 and 1/30 sec. ISO 100.

Cambrians Autumn

The small locality of Cambrians is actually near St Bathans in Central Otago, but this peaceful autumn scene deserved to be placed next to the one opposite. There is something special about a still autumn day where one can take the time to appreciate the colours and the quietness.

Nikon D810, 24–120mm at f13 and 1/15 sec. ISO 200.

INDEX

Previous spread

Arrowtown Colours

In mid/late April autumn comes alive in Central Otago, and Arrowtown is possibly the best place to see the magical colours. Here the whole hillside (apart from a few wild pines) is splashed with shades of yellow, orange and red.

Nikon D800E, 24–85mm at f8 and 1/125sec. ISO 100.

First published in 2019 by New Holland Publishers
Sydney • Auckland

Level 1, 178 Fox Valley Road, Wahroonga, NSW 2076, Australia
5/39 Woodside Ave, Northcote, Auckland 0627, New Zealand

newhollandpublishers.com

A catalogue record for this book is available from the National Library of New Zealand.

ISBN 9781869665210

Group Managing Director: Fiona Schultz
Publisher: Sarah Beresford
Editor: Elise James
Designer: Andrew Davies
Production Director: Arlene Gippert
Printer: Toppan Leefung Printing Limited

Cover image: Glenorchy Lagoon at Dawn
Endpapers: South Westland Mist
Back cover image: Ben Ohau Range

10 9 8 7 6 5 4 3 2 1

Keep up with New Holland Publishers:
NewHollandPublishers
@newhollandpublishers